Chimpanzees

Leo Statts

abdopublishing.com

Published by Abdo Zoom™, PO Box 398166, Minneapolis, Minnesota 55439. Copyright © 2017 by Abdo Consulting Group, Inc. International copyrights reserved in all countries. No part of this book may be reproduced in any form without written permission from the publisher. Abdo Zoom™ is a trademark and logo of Abdo Consulting Group, Inc.

Printed in the United States of America, North Mankato, Minnesota
062016
092016

Cover Photo: Gudkov Andrey/Shutterstock Images
Interior Photos: Eric Isselee/Shutterstock Images, 1; Shutterstock Images, 4–5, 12; Patrick Rolands/Shutterstock Images, 6; Eric Gevaert/Shutterstock Images, 7; Dave M. Hunt Photography/Shutterstock Images, 8; iStockphoto, 9, 15; Yves Grau/iStockphoto, 10–11; Red Line Editorial, 11, 20 (left), 20 (right), 21 (left), 21 (right); Gary Wales/iStockphoto, 13; Sam DCruz/Shutterstock Images, 14; Jeryl Tan/iStockphoto, 17; Kitch Bain/Shutterstock Images, 18; Kristof Degreef/Shutterstock Images, 19

Editor: Brienna Rossiter
Series Designer: Madeline Berger
Art Direction: Dorothy Toth

Publisher's Cataloging-in-Publication Data
Names: Statts, Leo, author.
Title: Chimpanzees / by Leo Statts.
Description: Minneapolis, MN : Abdo Zoom, [2017] | Series: Rain forest animals |
    Includes bibliographical references and index.
Identifiers: LCCN 2016941133 | ISBN 9781680791938 (lib. bdg.) |
    ISBN 9781680793611 (ebook) | ISBN 9781680794502 (Read-to-me ebook)
Subjects: LCSH: Chimpanzees--Juvenile literature.
Classification: DDC 599.885--dc23
LC record available at http://lccn.loc.gov/2016941133

Table of Contents

Chimpanzees

Chimpanzees are smart primates. They use tools like humans. The tools help them eat.

Chimps **communicate** in many ways.

They kiss and hug. They tickle, too.

Body

Chimps have big ears.

Their fur is black. It does not cover their faces, hands, or feet.

Habitat

Chimps live in Africa. Some live in rain forests. Others live in forests or grasslands.

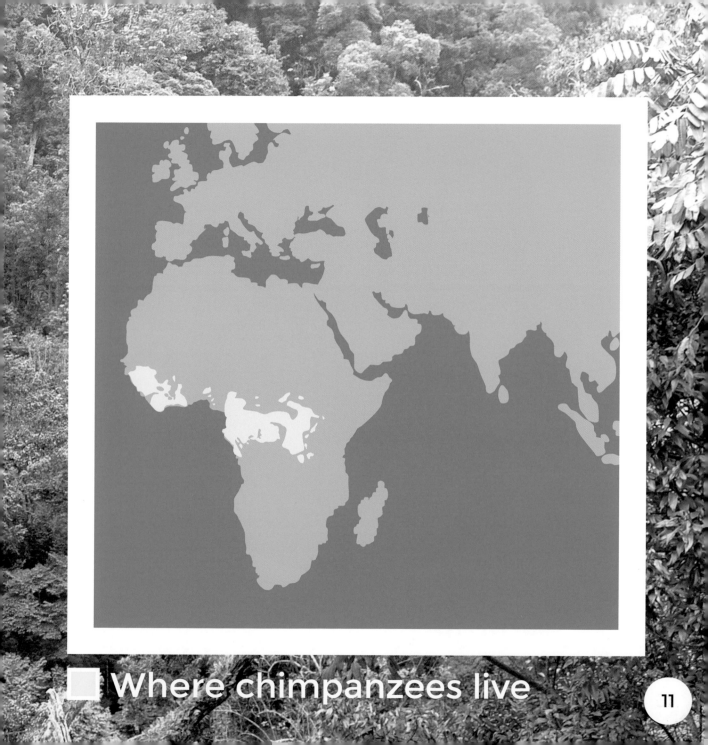

Where chimpanzees live

Chimps live in groups.
Some groups have 20 chimps.

Others have up to 150. Each group has a **territory**. They protect it from other groups.

Chimps mostly eat plants and fruit. They also eat nuts.

Chimps use rocks to open nuts.
They hit the nuts with a rock.
This cracks the nuts open.

Sometimes chimps eat small animals. They also eat insects. They dig for the insects with twigs.

Life Cycle

Chimps usually have one baby at a time. The baby rides on its mother's back.

It stays with her until it is two.
Chimps can live 45 years.

Quick Stats

Average Height

A chimpanzee is shorter than a door.

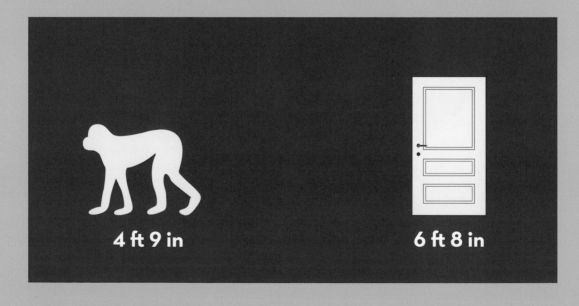

4 ft 9 in

6 ft 8 in

Average Weight

A chimpanzee weighs as much as a toilet.

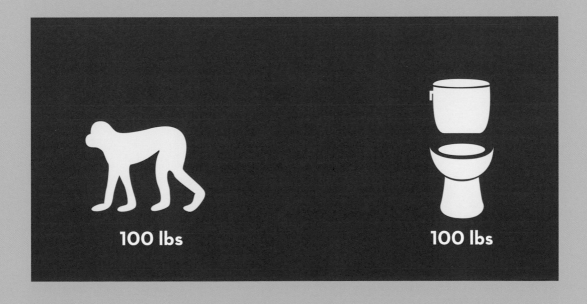

100 lbs   100 lbs

Glossary

communicate – to give and receive information.

grassland – a large area of grass, with few or no trees.

primate – a group of animals that includes humans, apes, and monkeys.

rain forest – a tropical woodland where it rains a lot.

territory – an area that animals live in and guard.

Booklinks

For more information
on **chimpanzees**, please visit
booklinks.abdopublishing.com

Zoom In on Animals!

Learn even more with the Abdo Zoom
Animals database. Check out
abdozoom.com for more information.

Index